Movie Stars
MEMORY LANE

By Hugh Morrison

Montpelier Publishing, London
2018

Follow us on Facebook

ISBN-10: 1723057983
ISBN-13: 9781723057984

Published by Montpelier Publishing, London
Printed and distributed by Amazon Createspace

ntroduction

o you remember Saturday night at the movies?
The mounting excitement as the lights dimmed?
ughing at the cartoons?
ating popcorn or hotdogs?
ishing the 'B' movie would end so you could watch the
ain feature'?
ow you can relive the magic of the movies with this book
out the stars of the golden age of Hollywood...

Silent Stars

Douglas Fairbanks, Snr

From the beginning of cinema around 1900 until the late 1920s, all films were silent, accompanied by music played by a pianist or a small orchestra.

Mary Pickford

Important dialogue was shown on the screen, but most of the story had to be portrayed through the expressions and actions of the players. Many of the old silent stars are forgotten now, but here are a few that are still quite well known.

Marlene Dietrich

Greta Garbo and John Gilbert

Lilian and Dorothy Gish

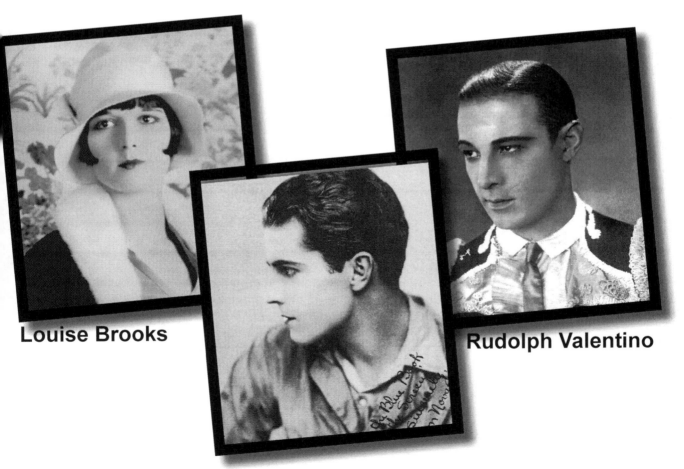

Louise Brooks

Rudolph Valentino

Ramon Novarro

LEADING MEN

Tyrone Power

The golden age of Hollywood introduced the world to a new type of leading man: handsome, debonair, impeccably dressed and well mannered, but able to look after himself (and his leading lady, of course) in a tight spot.

Here are some of the best loved leading men of the silver screen from the 1930s to the 1960s.

Ronald Coleman and Madeleine Carroll in *The Prisoner of Zenda*, 1937

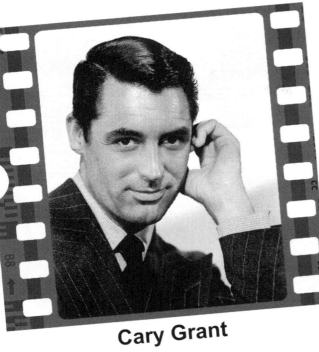

Cary Grant

Clark Gable and Vivien Leigh in *Gone with the Wind* (1939)

Above: Gregory Peck
Right: James Stewart

Leading Ladies

Marilyn Monroe in The Seven Year Itch, (1954)

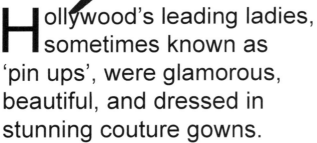

Hollywood's leading ladies, sometimes known as 'pin ups', were glamorous, beautiful, and dressed in stunning couture gowns.

Although some played the parts of 'dizzy blondes', many were smart, sophisticated and able to hold their own against the leading man. Here are some of the top leading ladies of cinema's old days.

Bette Davis

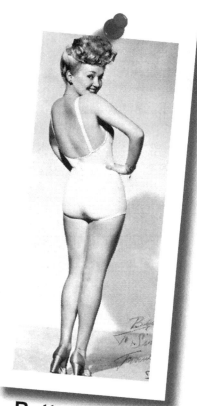

Betty Grable

Veronica Lake

Lauren Bacall

Audrey Hepburn

Elizabeth Taylor

Katherine Hepburn

Cops 'n' Robbers

Crime films were always popular, particularly stories about bootleggers, and gangsters, or murder mysteries.

The cops, private detectives and the FBI or 'G Men' were never far behind, and the crooks were nearly always caught, because 'crime does not pay'. Here are some of the stars of Hollywood crime movies.

James Cagney, probably the best known gangster actor.

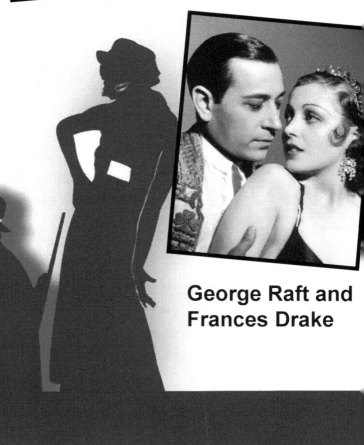

George Raft and Frances Drake

Edward G.Robinson (left) and Humphrey Bogart. Bogart played gangsters but also played the private detective Sam Spade

Basil Rathbone and Nigel Bruce, as the famous English detective Sherlock Holmes and his sidekick Dr Watson

elow: Robert tchum and Jane eer in the detective m *Out of the Past* 947)

Right: the Chinese detective Charlie Chan, played by Sydney Toler

Make 'em laugh!

Times were often hard in the old days, so what better way to forget your cares than to laugh them away at the movies.

Short comedy films and full length features kept the blues at bay, especially during the dark days of the Great Depression and World War Two.

Here are some of the most popular comic actors of Hollywood's golden age.

Buster Keaton

Harold Lloyd

Laurel and Hardy

Charlie Chaplin a 'The Tramp'

The Three Stooges

Groucho Marx

**Abbott
and Costello**

**Dean Martin
and Jerry Lewis**

Bob Hope

The Wild, Wild West

Right from the early days of cinema there have been movies about the Wild West, featuring cowboys, homesteaders, battles between Indians and the US Cavalry and of course, the 'shootout' on Main Street between two gunslingers.

Some of the best-known westerns of Hollywood's golden age include *High Noon* (1952), *Riders of the Purple Sage* (1941) and *Shane* (1953).

John Wayne and Ga[...] Russell in *Angel an[...] the Badman* (1947)

Left: Alan Ladd in *Shane* (1953)

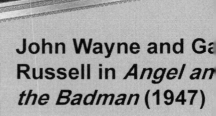

Roy Rogers and Gail Davis, 1948

Gene Autry, the 'singing cowboy'

Gary Cooper in *High Noon*, 1952

Tom Mix, the first movie cowboy

Child Stars

The movie business was not just for adults. Films starring child actors were very popular, particularly for families and for children who were often allowed to go to the cinema by themselves on Saturday mornings.

Many of the child stars of the old days are forgotten but several went on to act in adulthood, including Mickey Rooney and Elizabeth Taylor.

Jackie Coogan, one of the first child stars, with Charlie Chaplin in *The Kid* (1921)

*Our Gang
(The Little Rascals)*

Shirley Temple with her fans, 1938.
Shirley had a big hit with her song
On the Good Ship Lollipop

Mickey Rooney and
Judy Garland in *Love
Finds Andy Hardy*,
1938

Left:
Margaret
O'Brien in
*Journey for
Margaret*, 1944

Mickey Rooney and
Elizabeth Taylor in
National Velvet (1944)

Journey into Space!

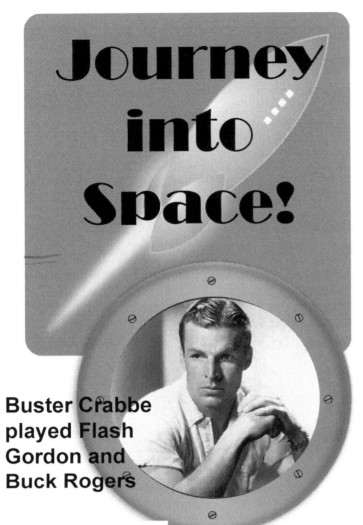

In the 1930s and 1940s science fiction movies, mainly about fantastic trips into space, became very popular, particularly in the form of Saturday morning serials for children featuring characters such as Flash Gordon and Buck Rogers.

In the 1950s as space flight became a reality, science fiction movies really took off, with hundreds of titles made, many on a low budget. Here are a few of the posters and actors of the genre.

Buster Crabbe played Flash Gordon and Buck Rogers

Michael Rennie starred in *The Day The Earth Stood Still* (1951)

Carmen D'Antonio and Charles Middleton in *Flash Gordon* (1936)

Leslie Neilsen and Anne Francis in *Forbidden Planet* (1956)

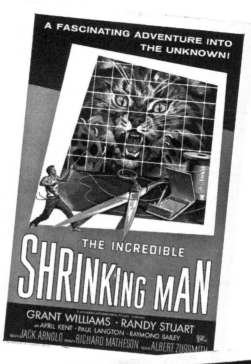

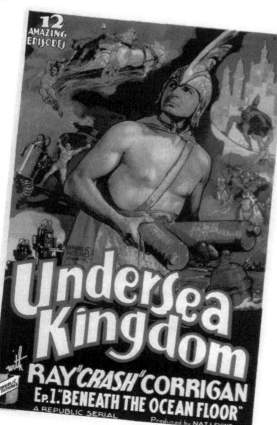

MUSICALS

The musical has been one of the most successful types of movie created by Hollywood.

Ever since Al Jolson became the first person to sing in the movies in *The Jazz Singer* (1927), music and dancing has been a vital part of family entertainment at the cinema.

Take a look at some of the big stars of Hollywood's top musicals of the 30s, 40s and 50s.

Tommy Dorsey in *The Fabulous Dorseys* (1941)

Grace Kelly and Frank Sinatra *High Society* **(1956)**

Doris Day starred in *Calamity Jane* (1953)

Singer Bing Crosby appeared in the *Road To...* musicals with Bob Hope

Howard Keel starred in *Annie Get Your Gun* (1950)

Singin' in the Rain (1952) with Gene Kelly and Debbie Reynolds

Fred Astaire and Ginger Rogers in *Top Hat* (1935)

The British are coming!

The golden age of cinema was not just about Hollywood. The British film industry produced many popular movies which did well both in the United Kingdom and the USA.

Many British stars made the journey to Hollywood to become completely Americanised – examples include Charlie Chaplin and Cary Grant – but others retained their distinctive British charm throughout their careers.

Above: David Niven in *Enchantme* (1948)
Left: Ronald Colman

Joan Collins and Ray Milland

Roger Moore

Dirk Bogarde

Sean Connery

urence Olivier
d Joan Fontaine
Rebecca (1940)

Elizabeth Taylor

**Above: Richard Burton
Left: Noel Coward**

FRIGHTFUL FILMS

Cinema audiences in the old days loved a good fright! Scary horror films were always popular, with characters such as Dracula and Frankenstein and a host of other ghouls and ghosts guaranteed to get cinema-goers shivering in their seats, breathing a sigh of relief as the lights went on again at the end of the show!

Lon Chaney in *The Phantom of the Opera* (1925)

The giant gorilla *King Kong* (1933)

Lon Chaney in *The Wolf Man* (1941)

Boris Karloff in
Frankenstein
(1935)

Bela Lugosi in
Dracula (1931)

Peter Lorre
appeared in
many creepy
movies

Vincent Price in *The
House on Haunted
Hill* (1959)

Right: horror
film poster, 1954

Animal Actors

Never work with children or animals – so went the old movie saying – but it did not stop people trying! We have looked at some child stars so here are some of the animal stars that movie audiences grew to know and love during the golden age of Hollywood.

Gene Autry appeared in many films with 'Champion the Wonder Horse'

Left: 'Trigger' the horse, with Roy Rogers and Lynn Roberts

'Lassie' was a popular movie dog

There were several films made featuring the horse 'Black Beauty'

...heeta' the chimp appeared in ...e *Tarzan* movies with Johnny ...eissmuller

Buster Crabbe with a lion in *King of the Jungle* (1933)

Troubled Youth

Movies featuring teenage rebels have been around for a long time; for example in the 1930s there was a popular series of films featuring teenage crime gang the 'Dead End Kids'.

Leo Gorcey (above) and Billy Halop (left) appeared in the *Dead End Kids* movies

It was not until the postwar era however that teen rebels really came into their own. Here are some of the moody youth stars from the golden age of cinema.

Elvis Presley starred in *Jailhouse Rock* **(1957)**

James Dean in
*Rebel Without a
Cause*, 1956

Montgomery Clift
played troubled
youths in several
films

Marlon Brando in
*A Streetcar Named
Desire* (1948)

Jack Nicholson's
first movie was
The Cry Baby Killer
(1958)

Joan Collins
played a teen
tearaway in
Cosh Boy
(1953)

WAR HEROES

Robert Mitchum and Debora Kerr in *Heaven Knows, Mr Allison* (1957))

War movies have always been popular. In the 1930s a few famous ones about the First World War were made such as *Journey's End* and *Dawn Patrol,* but it was not until during and after the Second World War that the genre really took off.

Hundreds of war movies were made in the 1940s and 1950s, packed with action, thrills and romance.

Lee Marvin in *Attack* (1956)

Left: *Journey's End* (1930) w David Manners, Billy Bevan and Colin Clive

Left: Richard Barthelmess in *Dawn Patrol* (1930)

Future US President Ronald Reagan appeared in several war movies

Steve McQueen appeared in *The Great Escape* (1963)

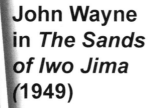

John Wayne in *The Sands of Iwo Jima* (1949)

Motorcycle ridden by Steve McQueen in *The Great Escape*

OTHER LARGE PRINTS BOOKS AVAILABLE FROM MONTPELIER PUBLISHING

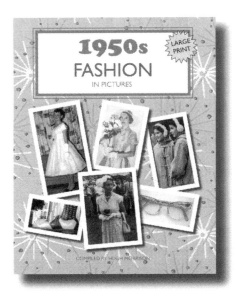

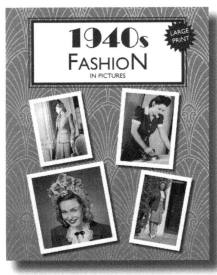

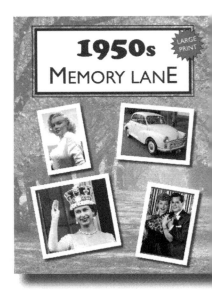

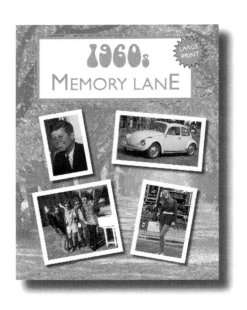

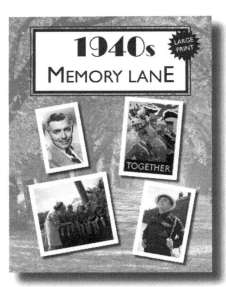

ORDER YOUR COPIES ONLINE TODAY!

Made in the USA
Coppell, TX
11 June 2020